Separation Anxiety

Sean Lause

ISBN: 978-81-8253-863-4

First Edition: 2022
Rs. 200/-

Cyberwit.net
HIG 45 Kaushambi Kunj, Kalindipuram
Allahabad - 211011 (U.P.) India
http://www.cyberwit.net
Tel: +(91) 9415091004
E-mail: info@cyberwit.net

Printed at VCORE CONNECT LLP..

For my son, Christopher, with love

Acknowledgements

I would like to thank Tom Beery and Will Wells for all their wise advice concerning my poems.

Poems in *Separation Anxiety* have appeared in the following journals:

"Soldier's Day"——*The New Verse News*

"The Exiled Menagerie"—-*FutureCycle Press*

"For Little Sister"—*The Dead Mule School of Southern Literature*

"David"—*Kaleidoscope*

"The Door"—F*utureCycle Press*

"Oh light inscrutable"—*The Write Place at the Write Time*

"The telescope's infinite longing"—*Miller's Pond*

"Bach on the radio"—*Haiku Headlines. Haiku Reality*

"The earth as crucifixion"—*FutureCycle Press*

"Seeling Night"—-*The Deronda Review*

Contents

Part One: Ulro

"Man has closed himself up, till he sees all things thro' narrow chinks of his cavern."

—William Blake, *The Marriage of Heaven and Hell*

Overheard in the Utopia Bar

"…he stifled an American scream."—
—John Berryman, Dream Song 211

I'm not wearing a fucking mask.
My freedom Trumps your fear!"
-
Fear? This boozehome
unstill in nervosities
commits coins to madness
like a paranoid jukebox,
while out a window high
a Tambo and Bones moon
moves like a cripple,
and witches appall the clouds.
"It's them Mexicans, it's them Jews,
it's them Muslims…"
It's those fibrillating Mugwumps,
alert to your heartless.
"Death to Obama! Public executions!"
Their words, words, words move in hateswarms,
infecting sight, as internet crickets
click out conspiracies, resentment grimace
and fear eyes travel the smoke
like nightmare spiders.
My head dizzies my alone and silent.
Their hate an evil purity, without regret.
Now each chooses an animal to become.
Beer is flowing.
The rats must be moving,
enraged as a wound in a raw wind.

Contents

Poems in *Separation Anxiety* have appeared in the following journals:

"Soldier's Day"——*The New Verse News*

"The Exiled Menagerie"—-*FutureCycle Press*

"For Little Sister"—*The Dead Mule School of Southern Literature*

"David"—*Kaleidoscope*

"The Door"—F*utureCycle Press*

"Oh light inscrutable"—*The Write Place at the Write Time*

"The telescope's infinite longing"—*Miller's Pond*

"Bach on the radio"—*Haiku Headlines. Haiku Reality*

"The earth as crucifixion"—*FutureCycle Press*

"Seeling Night"—-*The Deronda Review*

"The Jews will not replace us!
The Storm is coming!"
They stomp, whistle, howl, cry, bray,
roar, honk, bark and hiss,
then stridor outside,
lit with apocalyptic neon.
While I, to my drunken stupor shame,
say nothing.

Lima, Ohio, 2021

In the Town Square,
someone dressed as Spider-Man
screams at the rain: "Trump won!"
The shadow of the Allen County Jail
grows like a nearing giant
hungering for the poor.
In a sudden wind,
torn lottery tickets
vertigo the air
like wounded butterflies.
Parking lot, abandoned factories,
Confederate flags for sale
under Yankee skies.
Fire
s
c
a
p
e
s
down
e
m
p
t
y
businesses

I am hunting for the Ranger Theater.
Its back wall once beheld a Texas Ranger,
his six guns blazing at injustice.
But he is gone,
and I am lost in time and memory.

Girl on a bus

Who is this girl crying at the snow
and laughing
as it sings and swirls round the bus?
She presses her breath and hands to the glass,
as if to touch its innocence soft and cool,
and her reflection shares her wonder.
Some college boys in front
sing "Yellow Submarine,"
and peek at her and giggle.
Imagine then why she is crying.
We may never know for sure,
who were born and raised in cold weather.
Is it exclusion,
taunting words and songs
twisted from joy to cruel?
Or is it all the angels shattered
and scattered to earth,
to plant it with Winter seeds?
If the latter, it might be
like seeing snow fall
for the very first time.

My response to the Town Glee Club's mailed invitation to sing Christmas Carols in the square

Thank you, but no. These days
I am a citizen of somewhere else.
I am still faithful,
but reluctant and rather stubborn,
like Mother Mary's mule.
My body is not a beehive,
humming unity of time and place,
or even a tree draped in delirious color.
I'm too strangered to sing carillon unison
while I feel alien deep within.
Don't get me wrong, I'm all for glee,
but God rest me I can't keep it going
for long, not with—you know—crucifixions
in sight, and a community, by definition,
means somebody won't get to sing.

Between shocking falls

"Our Durlbin is sworming in sneaks."
—*Finnegan's Wake*

Listen carefully—
This time they could be our own.
Make ready—make the radar glow its emerald.
Betrayals blow like bats from wind to wind.
Put up the scenery—they like a show.
Pick some fat fool to lead them.
Let strategic paranoia work its will.
We need a tractable, usable rage.
Place our whispers winding through their ears.
A mosquito's cry will spook them.
And though every one of them owns a gun,
we've shipped their hands away.
We'll have their children for dessert.
Necessary murder drinks the blood of flowers.
They'll learn Ol' Marster's never wrong.
We know what's buried beneath the statues.

When Marvels abound

Dazzled pyrotechnic, we watch the helpless
civilians we are not, we refuse to be,
panic-run, not us, propped in our clock-
work seats, lid-locked, eyes glued, feet stuck
to the floor, stuffing popcorn down our darkness.
The Evil Mastermind strikes again!
Monster-Terrorist—the Other—we loathe and
fear, but then—zings in our Hero!
clenched in patriotic Spandex, cracking
wise his asides. We are saved again!
Law helpless, governments inept, stupid,
civilians impotent as extras—Wham!
Pow! Auk! Welcome a good clean sock
on the Devil's jaw. The Hero. We all know
his secret identity. He is us turned slayer.
Miracle! A sudden Authority! All we
need now a divine order, trial by combat,
send us in holy rage to the doors of the
Deep State, each his own superhero, dressed
to kill, till battered heads rattle like spit teeth.

Soldier's Day

The crowd cheers as the first line appears,
the summer's pride, like the sweet, brittle air
that lightning leaves in its wake,
their uniforms fresh and crisp,
their eyes brimming with visions
of harems whirling in honey sands.
Two wars against The Terror.
But now another line steps forth
with less assurance, hair tainted silver,
a look of shock twisted to grimace
that the betrayed often wear,
followed by a row of invisible men,
felt only by their absence, ghosts
of a forgotten war
But now the crowd excites, ecstatic
with beer and popsicles,
as the Good War survivors step by,
in their eyes a still nobility, flags wagging,
eyes bright as a Hellcat Fighter plane.
A brass band bangs by to end the parade—but
then come the un-invited——
and the crowd shivers silent
as before them creep the faded green
of Belleau Wood, faces like closed fists,
necks like wrinkled dough, bloody feet
stumping in mud that never leaves,
as they try to gum the words of a song
they no longer can remember.
And last, driving the coward crowd's retreat,

stagger the warriors of the Lost Cause.
The sun bleeds cancer bones. Overhead
hang the spent ghosts of wasted guns
and a star-crossed flag, blown with holes.
Their heads gleam like hysterical doorknobs.
Beast moans in hollow mouths, hands mere spiders,
their grey coats bleeding arrogance and sand.
And that night in all the town,
not one child dreamed of old renown.

Lynchmob Nobody

Lynchmob Nobody enjoyed his days.
Nothing could touch the darkness in his mind.
He was there at Salem and Sand Creek,
Washita, and there at Wounded Knee.
Watched Leo Frank strung from a tree.
At every blood-letting, Nobody was there.
He was there on the Night of Broken Glass,
watched the mob walk in fiery rings.
Philadelphia, Mississippi,
his white sheet ghosting in the wind.
Nobody was there, Nobody was witness,
as the blood escaped through the stars.
Then Nobody died in his Nobody town,
and when he was buried he only went down.
The minister was late, no crowd was there
to watch Nobody meet his last December.
The minister left and a shovel stuffed Nobody
in a grave that would never remember.

Look sharp, Lord

"Ó yes, at this point in time the American soul
gathers its forces for the good of man
but it has memories…the place is crawling
with ghosts."

—John Berryman

Look sharp, Lord.
Dark noons here come bleeding seriate,
dark cries doom down to ancient wounds.
Pitiless guns blasts our hearts to mournings.
Look sharp, Lord.
Death and Mercy, those lonely ones,
perceive what demons do,
that undream every song to silence.
Pain most unholy accurate,
where ghosts dance up and down our bones,
articulate in blindness, the nightmare
the madness crowd denies.
Here where manacled minds imagined lynching,
while hidden below, overwhelmed to men's eyes,
something comes crawling, breeding lies.
Lord, look sharp.

The sleeping Roma

I returned to my home town
to find it had undreamed itself
to the width of a needle tip
that drilled down my memory
to the bone, until nothing was
what I thought I once knew.
All the men were wanton boys,
their women open wounds.
Memories fled with ghosts of delirium,
and opioids floated mid-air.
The villagers pointed at me
and chanted in a tongue of hate.
All my abracadabras
toppled with the cards.
I became a cosmic Roma
beaten from my lands.
Rattling somewhere inside me
a heart I could no longer find.

The exiled menagerie

God is a gunpowder behind the eyes,
shot through the core of a desperate paradise.
When you catch the bullet in your teeth you will know
you are no longer lost in the circus.
Now you guess by the bearded lady's clues.
The artificial gypsy will bless your dreams with wolves.
You will learn to recite extraterrestrial alphabets
to the rhythm of the knife's near-miss.
All the whispered and tortured beasts
will guide your graceful taunts of gravity
as you watch your feet dare each other
across the wire—net-less, terrified, home.
You, prince of the circle of wounds.
You, priest of the exiled menagerie.

Poem sing only Blues

Poem sing only Blues
drawn from the deep wound.
Sing my dark blood awake,
sing all the lonely in my bones.
Poem sing only Blues
plunged to the deep sound,
sing the silence between two sobs,
that flows unknowing to the true.
Poem write the white part last.
Black notes go deeper, downer,
abandoned be to blue dimensions,
weaving dawn to seeling night.
Poem bend my heart to yearnings,
poem teach my heart to see.
Poem sing me only Blues,
poem send my soul to free.

Separation Anxiety

Wherever I look there's a door,
and light and life shut me out
like a line of dew
retreating before the sun.
At times I break through
so briefly, bleeding from everywhere,
but the silence returns each night,
forever faithful to its alone.
I stare at the world like a startled fish,
trapped inside its aquarium,
distorted to absurd dimensions,
dreaming of rivers and seas.
My words fail the winds,
like smothered butterflies
sink wings through soft clay,
a palimpsest of wounds.
I try to touch—
Everything strangers itself!
I am the cicada locked inside the shell,
and love may come when broken into free.

When dreams come altering the known

Come the dreams again, altering the known,
stalking their shadows past the witches
tittering in the trees. Stars appear,
seeking their forgotten names. They hover
like atrocities, incapable of speech.
The storm descends, cutting itself on stones.
I learn chants, sometimes screaming with the owls.
This is my home.
I own its every bone of silence,
lover of its songs and cries,
and its crows smooth-elusive in the night.
Here, where hallucinations gather grace,
where darkness blooms its mushrooms in my veins.
Oh what a smooth steel blade is moonlight!
And Venus and Mars are pure electroshock.
Here where memory rattles its box of
skeletons, and angels come in for the kill,
the wasp digs deep in my nested mind.
Watch me carve my heart down root by root,
for truth is blood that beats in longings.
I hear the near beasts gnawing on visions.

Let it crawl

You hear it in your basement deep at night,
at those odd, bent hours that never sleep,
hours that whisper unspeakable visions.
You can swear you hear it crawling.
It is.
Let it crawl.
Do not go down there.
Can't you see it possesses
an integrity no mere human
can comprehend? An eldritch
wholeness, blind as the dark side of the moon?
There it dreams the origin of night,
a darkness to teach the silence
how to scream.
Its blood pumps only nightmares.
Its eyes—has it eyes?
If so, they see right through you.
Perhaps it weaves designs of you
and you alone,
an image of purest ebony dementia
that will burn your deepest fear to reverence.

Part Two: Generation

"Without contraries there is no progression."

—William Blake, *The Marriage of Heaven and Hell*

Descend, descend...

No—descend, descend…
There is no way back to the garden
devoid of hands and feet, so learn
to crawl again, for what crawls still
lives, inward, downward, earthward
world-wording to heal the wound.
Till no more nowhere for us to be.
The hard-cold-brickness of this day
can be scaled below its walls.
No god of worth is known but inch-by-inch.
Prepare you a terrible redemption.

My father's headache

"Leave your father alone," my mother whispers.
"He has another headache."
"I'm fine," he mutters. "I'm not in pain."
He holds his head like a great weight of time.
He has turned the heat down in December,
sits by the empty living room table
in his old Winter overcoat,
whistling a song with no beginning or end,
his fingers quivering like frightened birds.
My mother's hands try to lead me away,
but I must stay—my breaths haunt the air.
Finally he stands, stares ahead—blind to me,
then fades—I hear him descend the basement stairs.
What heart am I?
Why do I fear to follow?
I hear the electric saw clear its angry throat,
spin its galaxy of twisted teeth
that thunder the floorboards beneath my feet,
then the scream of pine planks cut in two.
They sound like crucifixions.
And deeper still, beneath my grievings,
I hear my father's cries.

Shadow dance

Late nights, my father danced with a shadow,
the way he taught himself to dance,
and shave, and tie a tie,
he fatherless for once and all.
He was not alone.
I watched him, crouched and unseen,
and that shadow loved him dear,
mirroring his every move.
He did not smile or sing or even hum,
donned his death mask for a bow,
elegant as a new-laid corpse
spending its ghosts in empty pockets.
I close my eyes and see him still,
dancing with that hole, that cipher,
clutching it tight, each night, each night,
never knowing it was only his own.

My two fathers

Grandfather I never knew
patted my nine-year-old dad on the head,
said, "Pete, take care of your mother and brothers."
My father's name was Ken.
"I'm taking your sister—can't afford you"—
and went away to a fairyland
just this side of graves.
Years later, my mother awaits him
on their secret sycamore branch,
her feet dangling, yellow dress puffing
in the summer wind—His roadster
appears in a cloud of dust and desire,
side-door open—he says come on—where?
Anywhere but here. And they go to mysteries
I'll never see or even touch in dreams,
down the roads of a gone America.
The father I knew was broken in two,
undreamed of in hope or sunrise,
trapped forever between two worlds—
one endlessly lost in the past—
the other wounded each day in time,
his very words the phantoms of his silence.

Why Communism failed

Strive, strive, strive and succeed,
that endless, humorless, Puritan burden,
debts—faltering hearts and homes—children.
I watched one man return his son's one gift
for Christmas—clued him to life's harsh rule:
Children are a curse—dead weight—debts to fate.
The big strike in '62—Westinghouse,
my father refused the dole. Instead
he sold Whisk detergent door-to-door.
Whisk.
Hundreds of bottles stacked in our basement
like unemployed angels.
I remember the look in his eyes
of bitter-complete humiliation,
his eyes like rusty nails ripped from a wall,
the morning sun cold as a guillotine,
his best friend—laid off for good—shot himself
with a Luger he'd looted from the war.
Mrs. Hollib, the hole-puncher,
froze to death in her living room,
trying to save heat.
Her house had blinded eyes.
I saw the body—
the eyes frosted white.
On Christmas day, the snow
swirled round and back in undertow
while Karl Marx hid in the backyard shed.
It will not work, it will not work—here,
where the slaves all die without their slavery,
all their lives spelled down the bottom line.

My brother's photo album

My brother stands under a fisted sun,
posing, wincing a smile, his lips
thirsting for kisses—anything—a girl,
a leaf, a quiver of moon—but nothing
comes, and the wet stones reek like rotting fish.
His eyes dream of teeth strong and tender enough
to bite his virginity to the bone.
His eyes stare straight through the lens
like pummeled nails. His heart cries
like the shadow of a wounded crow.

My brother stands under a hollow moon,
impersonating all of Andersonville,
except he can not, will not eat, though
his hunger feeds and feeds on my heart.
The spider stars sting him so purely,
even his breaths are wounds.
I would take his picture but nothing is there,
he the final magician, in love with the
invisible.
Poems are no food for the truly hungry.
Brother, forgive your flesh.
Brother, you've got to love your Popeye.
Brother, my brother, you are all of you.

For little sister

You have found the secret place,
this baptism, this white chalice,
where Clytemnestra webbed her vengeance,
where a traitor screamed as a blind girl
sang all loss, where we all come, soon
or late, when the world enforces whispers.
This confession chamber, chancel, where
I shed and blessed my first menstrual blood.
Here where no shame need abide in wounds,
where silver needles sting the pain awake
and drown it, and the drain removes the clues.
Here your tears come all chameleon.
Here your pain forgives your silence,
and your body quivers with fear and longing,
yet sets your cry free, whole in its circle of rain,
your words, unsealed till the end of time. Let
go. No one will know. No one will ever know.

David

In my eyes, he still watches me
in dreams suspended
from dusty mirrors.
His head a broken drum,
born at a twisted angle,
as if some god of spite
snapped it to one side
before hurling him into the world,
his eyes question marks, his bony arms
pointless exclamations.
When he was a boy, the other boys
chased him, stoned him, but I
snapped my big slingshot
and drove them away.
Listen: I did something.
Sometimes I'd follow him unseen, unheard,
through secret paths behind the lockers,
listening for his breaths, his hands thrusting
the dark like wingless birds.
Mr. White, World History and Gym,
had clichés caught in his moustache.
He tossed them every day at David.
Be a man, David. Number Two is the first
Loser, David. Stop being a Dork, David.
Stop being the Hebrew Crip.
If had only cured cancer or killed himself,
I could be done with him perhaps.
But he only traced his loveless down the halls,
while in my dreams he forever turns away,
descending into a storm of silence.

Lost in Modern Fiction

Not one book can speak her true.
She is too beautiful for me in my alone.
She grabs me in the school library—
Cries—"Kiss me! Kiss me now!"
I swallow a gasp—nearly stutter—
No—I'm ugly and riddled with lust.
"I could EAT you!"
No—I'm too skinny—all the nuns say.
"Now's your chance! I'm yours!"
Second Floor, Aisle Two, Modern Fiction—
I'm terrified. What if it's a trap?
If I try to kiss her and she—pulls away and laughs?
Then tells everyone? I already hate myself now.
One trick like that, I'd hurl myself over
this railing like a teenage Frollo.
I'm too bewitched to speak, I turn away,
hear her cry from miles away—
"Oh, come back."
And I do not know, must know, cannot know—
though all I do is want and want—
where is truth—I escape to the stairs—
breathless, bookless, loveless and alone.

The approximated one

Under crocodile skies,
clocking and unclocking our days,
we memorized the numbers of our fates.
I hated them, those blind and empty numbers,
that abacused our lives with curses.
Joe Hunley, whose 92 I.Q. consigned him
to McNamara's "Idiot Brigade," zipped
and sealed in a body bag, Mekong '66.
Russell Malheur, fifty years at Dow Chemical,
his inner organs crawling with cancers.
Tommy Null, beaten to death by 1-2-3 white
cops, Detroit, '67, while we waited in the
school gymnasium to hear our draft numbers
float from loudspeakers—who stays, who goes,
who will turn into a gold star. All the boxes
returned to only our neighborhood on the wrong
side of the tracks, on the wrong side of everything.
They had our number sure. For every one of us,
a hundred deaths lay ready to subtract us.
A fine chance we had, rolling our eyes
out with the dice, casting our lots to tears,
counting our breaths down to zero.

Doomed for an uncertain term

One is left of four and that is math
never erased.
You are gone yet somehow I
feel the severed one.
How small the world turned to memory.
I keep its heart locked deep inside.
Leaves litter this path with wounds,
while the yew tree keeps trying to say.
I keep tripping over time,
pick up a phone to call one of you,
then memory returns your every absence.
Speak to me now. Tell me what silence sees.
In this dying Fall I am all and nothing.
I learn to grieve from the calling winds.
Crossing a deserted schoolyard I see
a single swing dancing with your ghosts.

It was when

It was when the steering wheel despaired of death,
when the rain through her rolled-down window
became her sudden tears from somewhere, tears
she licked to taste the salt of living.
It was when her car dreamed of horizons,
while she parked in a side street somewhere,
and the windshield wipers listened,
repeating lost mantras, sticking,
while her heart beat in rhythm with her cries.
It was when the cop prowled up to watch her—
then walked to her car who are you why
are you here, what do you think you're doing?
And someone said "I don't know."
It was then she knew she'd fallen into time,
halfway to tombstones and no way back
to innocence, and love, love, what are you
anyway, weaving this marriage to pain?

Toledo Amtrak pondering divorce

Art Deco tomb Friday one a.m.,
the whole train derailed outside Chicago.
Down in the Amtrak station,
I'm watching myself die.
I must not be seen by anyone happy.
I have forgotten my part.
One word might knock my sanity
Humpty Dumpty down,
so I am tolerant of silence,
and find deep comfort in shadows.
This city of glass
subsists on spit teeth,
and dismembered newspapers
strewn like drunks along the floors.
Hairless mannequins stare at nothing,
discarded like Dachau ballerinas,
bodies and bodies and bodies…
I know the body is holy,
but mine's become a thing I can't abide,
a bumbling Frankenstein scaring the peasants.
I want it chased and burned back to origins.
An old man's voice on the loudspeaker
says: "The train can't be fixed, the train's
gone stark steel mad, demolishing farms
with its dragon tail, the train, the train…"
I resist my obituary on the restroom wall.
Raincoats flutter like pinned butterflies.
I want to say "Look! The trains are filled with angels!
And Toledo is Heaven after all!"

But the train comes at last, as it must,
and I watch the Conductor lower the blinds,
while mushrooms the size of pillows
bloom up my legs and arms to the train,
all over the wedding car

The antique children

The antique children
are lined like convenient deaths
on a Victorian love seat
in my Grandmother's store in the country.
Their eyes are jewels that glitter sinister moons,
apricot cheeks, but foreheads cracked with time,
their smiles dinched long ago, lips parted, mouthing
a silence—plump, prettied and alone.
I believe they are gifted, clued to the dark,
hands clutching an emptiness like gold.
Have they ever touched daylight?
Is there some memory they cannot say?
Late at night I hear them
walking from aisle to aisle,
awkward, desperate as asylum echoes,
searching for any door.
I cover my ears and try not to scream,
as their intricate fingers claw at my lock,
while their rocking horse, strung from the ceiling,
rides away, rides away, rides away…

Rachel

Is she a conversation with herself,
a hieroglyph of wounds?
She's cut and cut her precious arms
meant to enfold the world.
They've taken her penknife away,
and left her in this silence,
and yet her body sings,
must sing, or she may die.
We're both on three-day hold,
though no one's holding us.
un-resurrected, danger to ourselves,
if we know what selves we be.
Childhurt—what demon pushed
you from the Lifetree to this place?
A spider, webbed in a window,
plays on her mournful strings.

Student Night at the Pizza Planet

The room speaks all its noise to itself,
excluding her.
She cannot spin or weave it to cohere.
Eyes float out and around, seeking smiles.
She's all and only one curled in a booth,
silent and invisible.
She tries to push a smile up—no good.
Theirs come so briskly white.
She ponders how and why.
Outside the purpling steamed window,
a little star peers twinkle twinkle.
Off in a bent mirror, she spies her outer self.
To Hell with it—true to Autumn winds
she blows right out the door, where she
spins, sings to the coming night
her own song—lovely and bare and pure.

Part Three: Heaven in a Wild Flower

"To see a World in a grain of Sand
and a Heaven in a Wild Flower
Hold Infinity in the palm of your hand
and Eternity in an hour…"

—William Blake, "Auguries of Innocence."

Schizophrenia vs. haiku

This wind
in love
with her hair.

Cat
watching moonlight
on the floor

How-to, how-
to-how-to-
sings the redbird

Mending a shirt—
This too
my mother taught me.

The rain gone,
sparrows
sip from a puddle.

This old man
tending his garden
lets one weed live.

Winds blowing the words
free
of the pine tree

The same moon
Basho saw,
the same moon.

Sixty today—
the dandelion heads
have also turned silver.

Three kites—
one green, one blue,
one too far away to tell.

Bach on the radio—
A spider weaves her web
with furious joy.

Wicked blackbird!
Why have you plucked the berry
red as her lips?

Let them call—
the tree frogs…
They're lonely too.

A cotton tree seed
traces its shadow
down the sidewalk.

This old hammer,
and these nails—
my father taught me how.

Wedding night,
her feet
so warm.

The door

A monarch butterfly,
freshly unwoven,
glitters with uncertainty,
clings to my front door knob,
shivers, pulses, watches
me with its needle eyes.
If I open the door,
it may tumble and scatter
like burning paper.
And it is burning,
burning with light,
burning with time
and possibility, and so
I keep the door closed,
waiting for this presence to
turn from the green of all imagining
to the blood of all ascent,
thrust into oneness like a heart,
wounding the air with its wings.
We both know how much this means.
Compared with it, the crucifixion needs
explaining. Yet it is as beyond me
as flight. I am no citizen of clouds.
Two wanderers then.
One seeking home, the other
its rightful kingdom of winds.
And so we wait as long as is given
an everyday miracle to suffice.

How the snail deals with painful memories

She winds them round and round herself
until they become her own internal spring,
until she is the ear of all echoes
that cannot hurt her here
where she binds life and death,
wound and grace, till she is rock and
stone and sea and wind woven
in her tight embrace, a whole universe
in miniature, spun to musings
that move her, inch-by-inch,
to a destination only patience knows.

Dogs and men

As a child I saw
a dog hit by a car.
His blood shot up,
trying to get back to heaven,
and I saw eternity
was hopelessly far and hopelessly near.
Animals know a way in
and a way out
of time,
passing through invisible doors,
moving between silences
like stars through clouds.
The suffering of animals
is complete, perfect, everywhere.
Their blood conspires with ours.
The dog tied in the snow—
It turns to bark North.
It turns to bark South.
But we have lost the language of their bones.
Dogs, men,
walk in rhythm when they are old,
careful, close to the earth,
each bone unbending pain,
shuttered, like we are seeing them
through gaps of light in a passing train.
That was my dog died that day,
and every day since,
blood it shed for me, so I could see.
The day you finally learn

you live and die in the breaths of others,
there may be nothing left to do
but build a circle in a grove of trees
and shout "I'm alive! I'm still alive!"
until winds weave an answer to the rain.

My Black Cat

I awake to her eyes in my eyes, mine in hers,
green eyes that pierce my blood and marrow—
her placid-perfect insistent-silent vigil,
crouching center of all my surrounds,
claws kneading me from dreams to sunrise.
Knows what she knows, wants what she wants,
this clinging weight on chest, heart, breath—
tail autographing the air, this football-
sized rememberer, pulsing shadow, this poem
in purr and fur—must be fed again.

The earth as crucifixion

I had a thirst to buy a crucifix
from fear, not love.
A sudden terror I awoke with
that I was about to go out
like a pinched candle.
That I would be nothing but a name.
I searched in store after store.
No cross. Found necklaces
strung with skulls, razors, clocks,
glocks, pentagrams, smiley faces.
No cross. Finally found one
in a souvenir shop. Plastic, it shattered
and scattered like sterile seeds.
I broke down, my bones sobbing.
"I'll be your crucifix,"
said dragonfly,
and spread his wings through the dying sun.

"I'll be your crucifix,"
said snake,
and pushed through his old skin to new.
"I'll be your crucifix,"
said deer,
and showed me her gaping wound.
And then I saw the world as crucifixion.
And every living thing a Christ.
Not one spared the spear.
The heart alone the Paraclete,
descending in dovelight.

Seeling Night

At times, the road below
pulled past endlessly
until I could feel the turns ahead,
and my head swayed with the creaking lamp,
my wings bound, eyes encased in black,
the night eternal,
only the church bells to remember.
Once I heard
the cat approach, withdraw, approach again.
I could smell its sweet breath
and hear the hunger in its claws
nearing my throat.
It spared me from fear, I think,
knowing what I am.
All around me was what I used to fear.
Crashing glass, cruel laughter,
the chink of coins, angry oaths,
words that bit the air,
whips snapping,
horses shrieking,
drunken men my owners—
until you came.
I almost surrendered
to exhaustion, thirst,
their mocking cries,
and the dark within the dark.
Now I feel your careful fingers
loose the thread at last.

The night withers,
and my eyes crave the light of lights.

Ascending, master of heights,
I follow my cries
to my pride of place—
A blue no man can see.
I journeyed, dying,
across eternities,
reborn at last
in the bend of my beating wings.

The "water-witch"

Her divining rod Ariels the wind,
seeking the holy center deep below.
One flick of the stick's bright tongue
and her quest will be complete.
The owner and the neighbors follow
at a slight, distrustful distance.
One spindly old woman points to her head
and mouths one word: "Touched!"
Dark below, the water stirs with longing,
for it is incomplete without a thirst.
The stick mesmers the wind to stillness,
and then it——lowers to the greening earth.
A sudden light ignites the air.
Her palms bleed, she faints in the waiting grass.
The neighbors gasp, the Baptist minister
prays that he need not touch her.
The divining rod claws the ground.
The tree roots quiver, sense an end to drought.
The owner jerks a thumb back,
and the steam shovel curses into life.

The wind that blows beyond our knowing

I like a wind without direction,
sent from gods of delirium,
that turns the treetops green to white
as if confessing their secrets.
That swirls the branches to a dance
of yes and no at once,
beckoning to us a yearned embrace,
random chance or fated grace.
A wind that won't or can't explain
the song that is its lover.
A wind like a mad magician's wand
that changes each to other.
Felt along one's nerve ends,
invisible as alone,
at once a rage for wandering free,
and for returning home.

Come Autumn

Come Autumn,
leaf-shimmering,
wind-wandering,
wing-flights freeing horizons,
day-moon wondering in blue—
let all your fallings spend the earth in gold.
Come, Autumn,
even in your tattered November dress,
and wind my thoughts to memories,
until I learn to listen to your silence
as it spills from leaf to leaf, and learn to hear
your gold and black
panther,
softly purring in the dark.

Song of the oak tree

Wand and harp, you
incandescent tree of
veins and longings,
you wave the winds into light,
dare the Fall to wounds
as your children leave you one by one,
and your roots seek deeper knowings,
rooted in clutch and thirst of memory,
your subterranean meditations
thread the dreams of the dead
that cling your forever to the earth.

Be

Be spider of weave and patience.
Be grave and learn what darkness sees.
Be root to reach depths beyond the mind.
Be light to catch reflection's thought,
and moon to cast shadows to a glow,
be glint in rat's eye—meaning of war.
Be hands to brush stars to longing.
Be heart to pulse your blood to life.
Be flesh and bone to sense the spirit with.
Let Autumn winds guide your words to free.
You'll be but you till you find the mirror
that reflects what it cannot see.

Oh light inscrutable

The splendor of my isolate city
that I carve from ice and snow,
this relentless Winter of “63—
I delve deep beneath the woeful tombs
of ancient winters, those pale kings.
I listen for emanations deep below,
seeking the icicle’s captured priest,
and my own enraptured heart.
Scrawling fables on the wounded winds,
molding the solstice to diamonds, I dig
deep, deeper still, tossing white plumes,
the snow humped high and higher,
to keep sure my secret world.
Then deeper yet, into the hard ground
of things, where the dark worm
keeps cold vigil for the Spring’s blood,
a hole cut in the top just wide enough for dreams,
so I can watch the stars snake-eye across the sky.
Outside howl the nearing wolves of war,
but here no hungered rage can find me,
nor the storm’s last shattered glass,
nor blundering giant batter down my door.
Oh light inscrutable,
with your snow’s swift slight-of-hand,
accept an old man’s incantation
to this sacrament of time.

How grammar invented the stars

Each star blooms its own enlightenment,
yet longs for a word to speak it.
Each planet circles its own imagining,
awaits a word to bend it round a god.
The new moon cups an old faith,
holding her child in her embrace,
dreaming our world round her reflections,
teaching night to glow with grace.
And we? We are satellites,
sending our messages through endless space.
Set your radio dial to zero,
then listen for deep returns.
Can you feel it now?
The way words bind the Zodiac of Fate?
Like a night in love with its own whispered light,
winding time to eternity.

How to watch a meteor shower

They come like wings—no—like light around
Eyes, mind open, waiting.
birdwings in flight, chanceled stars, flowering
sapphire incarnations, and we alone in
night's embrace all blessed with fireflies
suturing the darkness whole, breathless in
the grace of grasses, eyes widening to
admit the universe, the moon a silent
O of wonder.
They come like strings strumming
The Zodiac cannot guide you.
the night's guitar, shivering the
A meteor comes all in now.
tambourine moon, our "Ah!" in-
breath, inscape, more pure than prayer
or rush of bells through crystal air.
Down paths of ecstatic fire and sand,
Here the sky's ocean unfathoms
return time to eternity in grateful quest,
the night.
the moon a silver coin worth all spending.
They come, pulsing blood and agony
Try not to guess. This is like
shed for us, gold and silver snakes,
worrying one line of a poem
holy outriders of the Fall
till you ruin the whole.
that briefly bare the sky-blue gentian,
while high, high above all longing,

the moon's a gentle compass rose of love.
Let them plunder the light from darkness,
Do not worry about time. There
and carve an answer to the silence.
Is nothing to transend.
Thou gatherest here your sighs to angels,
the moon a sudden chrysalis
weaving the skeins of time.

The telescope's infinite longing

The sky cools to dark blue crystal
from the red-fisted rage of day.
Planets appear, swell to ripening grapes.
Alone, the telescope's widening eye
gathers the sheaves of light,
Glittering snakes striate the sky
with diamond eyes and ruby tongues,
while the night gently yields its constellations.
Tilted back in wonder, the world spins round
the scope's sure eye. Will we discover
what orbits dream? Its longing listens
to darkness breathing.
The sundial prays to the moon, then
time collapses, a magician's cane,
and death, a last, languid flower,
comes floating to the shores of heaven.

The map that love abandoned

A hole in this map
peers deeply through me,
hinting somewhere paper merely hides,
free of borders, free of compass
not the heart, free of same old folded
destinations, traced in arteries of ink.
I poke my pencil through, turning and
widening, a peephole in the Ozdoor,
hinting a strange world of blooms and plumes,
in wizard colors of the new, a hint
of somewhere near and far
that I may have for merely dreaming.
And now I tumble through the hole,
afloat to another world
where I feel home for first and last,
and held, truly held and this is my
heart beatlng like wings to another,
deep in the blue within the blue.

Become what you are

Listen.
The roots are whispering to your heart
unfathomed
beneath all meanings
the plot involves us
like autumn leaves quivering
the invisible
or undisastered stars
may guide you mystic to another.
Touch.
We are not separate.
Each wind dares our hands climb branches,
brush stars like dandelions
cast their Autumn ghosts to memory.
Look.
Your shadow awaits you, put it on.

The night the lights came

"It appeared—in vivid fire, with shining colors and balanced patterns—and released me from every thrall, inner and outer."

—Philip K. Dick, *Exegesis* 5:14

As a boy I was much afraid of all—
my haunted father, angry teachers,
monsters plotting in my closet,
swallowing their shadows, blasting caps,
tornadoes, atomic bombs and bullies.
Afraid too of my own sinful body,
confessing once a week in an upright coffin
to an invisible eye and a jealous ear
to a Minister of Fear, to a sinister
God of Sundays alone.
My mother would drape a blanket over
my bedroom mirror, to hide the lame boy
who came to me there each night, beckoning,
or tie a string to my wrist
to keep me from floating out the window.
Most of all I was afraid I'd disappear
like a magician's cane stunned into smoke,
or fold up like Alice's telescope,
tumble down an endless well of tears,
or fade out in dying whispers.
And then one night the lights came,
like animate seeds of longing.
They came glowing, glittering red

and gold—like the dreams of dragonflies,
weaving my heart to visions.

They came like rows of electric ants,
or patient illuminations of blood,
pulsing the air with living light,
their generous, loving irradiations
flowing through my veins.
The fearful world collapsed—a shattered
mirror—disappeared in light.
For once I was not alone.
For once I was not afraid.
I knew I could die and all is well.
For two weeks they guided me to sleep each night,
teaching me to see.
Each morning my eyes were glued shut.
My mother spat on her fingers and pried them
open—I still feel her fingers on my eyelids.
The lights never returned, yet
they taught me to dream of better worlds,
free from fear, free from darkness,
and I pray that deep within they guide me still,
with their sweet harmonious delirium of song.

Blessings of the fallen world

I'm healed and headed out the door
to this fallen world my home,
free of masks, free of fear,
no more ghosting in my own good skin.
I may even head downtown, wave my crazy
book around, risk old heartache and despair,
sing hallelujah what the hell,
or carve my name in the trembling air.
I have a secret history to reveal,
inked in blood and memory,
a pure premonition—like bird wings
know flight before the bird.
My mind to plummet, my heart raze pure,
unstrangering whatever I touch,
and in this broken time and place,
find somewhere near to whole.
"Tell the story," nods the oak,
"Send words as leaves to meanings."
Winter says: "A fence in a snowfield
divides nothing from itself."
"Time to make ready," says cicada.
"Spell your songs out one by one.
Hear my feet deep inner-earth—
I'm digging for the sun."

Coda

American Scream

Watch them Calibaning their hateful plots.
We made this monster, dreamed it into birth.
Its darkness must be owned.
We must scream an American Scream.
Let poets be God's spies, reporting to angels
how the past prologues us, psychotic
as shattered glass. Scream an American Scream
before the mobs burn our city on the hill.
Scream before silence descends its night.
Let bell-tongues tell of ancient horrors
returned, like worms oozing from the brain.
Speak healing truth deep down through the wound.

www.ingramcontent.com/pod-product-compliance
Lightning Source LLC
Chambersburg PA
CBHW022202160726
48282CB00024B/295
* 9 7 8 8 1 8 2 5 3 8 6 3 4 *